# Weird Friends

## Unlikely Allies in the Animal Kingdom

### Jose Aruego and Ariane Dewey

Gulliver Books

Harcourt, Inc.

San Diego    New York    London

For Juan
—J. A. and A. D.

Requests for permission to make copies of any part of the work should be mailed to
the following address: Permissions Department, Harcourt, Inc.,
6277 Sea Harbor Drive, Orlando, Florida 32887-6777.

www.harcourt.com

Gulliver Books is a trademark of Harcourt, Inc., registered in the
United States of America and/or other jurisdictions.

Library of Congress Cataloging-in-Publication Data
Aruego, Jose.
Weird friends: unlikely allies in the animal kingdom/Jose Aruego and Ariane Dewey.
p.   cm.
"Gulliver Books."
1. Symbiosis—Juvenile literature.   [1. Symbiosis.]   I. Dewey, Ariane.   II. Title.
QH548.A78   2002
577.8'5—dc21   2001001154
ISBN 0-15-202128-0

First edition
H G F E D C B A
Manufactured in China

The illustrations in this book were made with pen and ink, gouache, watercolor,
and pastel on Strathmore Kit paper.
The display type was set in Spumoni.
The text type was set in Stone Informal.
Color separations by Bright Arts Ltd., Hong Kong
Manufactured by South China Printing Company, Ltd., China
This book was printed on totally chlorine-free Nymolla Matte Art paper.
Production supervision by Sandra Grebenar and Pascha Gerlinger
Designed by Lydia D'moch

Many of the animals featured in this book
have weird names. Try these pronunciation tips:

anemone (a-NEM-a-nee)

rhino (RYE-no)

egret (EE-gret)

goby (GO-bee)

phalarope (FA-le-rope)

mackerel (MACK-rel)

Portuguese (POR-che-gheez)

labeo (la-BAY-o)

wrasse (RASS)

tuatara (TOO-a-TAR-a)

Sometimes in the wild, animals you might think could hurt each other actually help each other in surprising ways. They share food or a home. They warn one another of approaching predators. They cluster side by side for protection. Some animals even give others a good bath. Their survival often depends on these weird friendships.

# The Clown Fish and the Sea Anemone

The bright little clown fish needs protection from its enemies. So it chooses a poisonous sea anemone to be its bodyguard. For about an hour, the clown fish carefully darts in and out of the anemone's deadly tentacles. Little by little, it becomes immune to their sting. Then it moves in. The clown fish is safe from predators. So is the anemone, because its enemy, the butterfly fish, is afraid of the clown fish's bite.

# The Rhino and the Cattle Egret

As they graze across the plains, a rhino and her calf stir up grasshoppers. But the rhino can't see very well and may not notice danger approaching. So she lets a sharp-eyed cattle egret perch on her back to act as a lookout. The egret is rewarded with an endless feast of grasshoppers.

If the egret spies danger, it screams. And if *that* doesn't get the rhino's attention, it taps on the rhino's head until the mother and baby gallop to safety.

# The Blind Shrimp and the Goby

One species of shrimp is completely blind. But it knows how to get help. It digs a hole in the sand, crawls in, and waits for a goby fish to swim in for shelter. The goby has a place to hide, and the blind shrimp has a guide to lead it when it's safe to go out.

While they're feeding, the shrimp's antennae feel the goby's every move. If a predator approaches, the goby flicks its tail, and the two swim quickly back into their safe burrow.

# The Ostrich and the Zebra

Ostriches have terrific eyes. Zebras have terrific ears. When the two get together, nothing can sneak up on them. That's why ostriches and zebras often roam the savanna together, chomping on seeds and grasses.

The ostriches look, and the zebras listen, for predators. The first to detect a hungry lion warns the others, and before it can attack, they all flee to safety.

# The Red Phalaropes and the Sperm Whale

The red phalaropes follow a pod of sperm whales as they swim far out to sea. The birds hover over the water and wait for a whale to come up for air.

As soon as a whale surfaces, the birds land on its back and begin to pry parasites from cuts and cracks in its skin. Being free of these pests makes the whale feel better, and the phalaropes enjoy a tasty meal. But the birds have to eat quickly, because once the whale blows, it takes a breath, slaps its tail, and dives deep into the ocean.

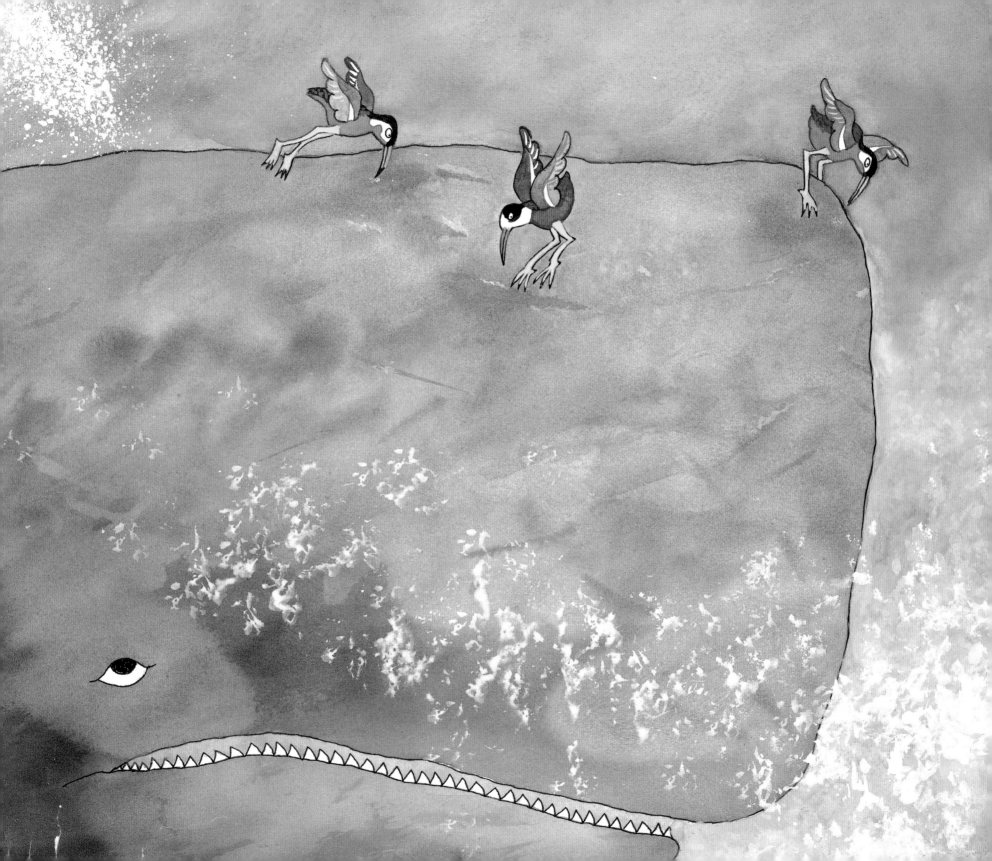

## The Red Ants and the Large Blue Butterfly

When red ants find a particular type of caterpillar, they lug it back to their nest. There, they tickle its tummy till it oozes the sweet honeydew they love to sip. In return, the ants feed the caterpillar all it can eat. The caterpillar lives unharmed in the ants' nest for eleven months, eating and pupating. Finally, it emerges as a Large Blue Butterfly, shakes out its wings, and flies away. Soon, the ants will go in search of another caterpillar.

# The Hermit Crab and the Sea Anemones

When a hermit crab needs a new home, it finds an empty shell, moves in, and sticks sea anemones on top for protection. The anemones' stinging tentacles scare away octopuses, which love to eat hermit crabs. Anemones can't walk, so the crab provides them with transportation to new feeding spots. And because crabs are messy eaters, there are always food scraps for the anemones to nibble.

# The Impalas and the Baboons

At the water hole, a herd of delicate impalas stays close to a troop of tough baboons. The impalas use their excellent senses of smell, hearing, and sight to detect danger.

If the impalas notice a predator approaching, they dance nervously. That warns the baboons, who bare their fangs and snarl to scare the attacker away.

## The Horse Mackerel and
## the Portuguese Man-of-War

When the horse mackerel is pursued by an enemy, it races for home.

The mackerel's home is a colony of small organisms living together called a Portuguese man-of-war. It has venomous ribbons that can reach seventy feet long and that shoot paralyzing, barbed harpoons into whatever they touch. But they don't harm the horse mackerel, because it doesn't feel their sting. The mackerel is safe and the man-of-war is well fed, because any predator that comes too close will end up as the man-of-war's dinner.

# The Forest Mouse and the Beetles

At night, the forest mouse scampers around the rain forest looking for food, with beetles clinging to its fur and face. But the mouse doesn't mind, because the beetles eat the fleas that infest its fur. During the day, while the mouse sleeps, the beetles dismount and eat the bugs in the mouse's burrow. The beetles are always well fed, and the mouse and its house are free of itchy insects.

# The Hippo, the Oxpeckers, and the Black Labeo Fish

The hippo can't scrub itself, so it wades into the river and waits for oxpeckers to land on its back. These birds peck off and eat ticks and other bothersome bugs. Meanwhile, in the water below, black labeo fish gobble up anything clinging to the rest of the hippo. When all the parasites have been removed, the hippo naps in the cool mud.

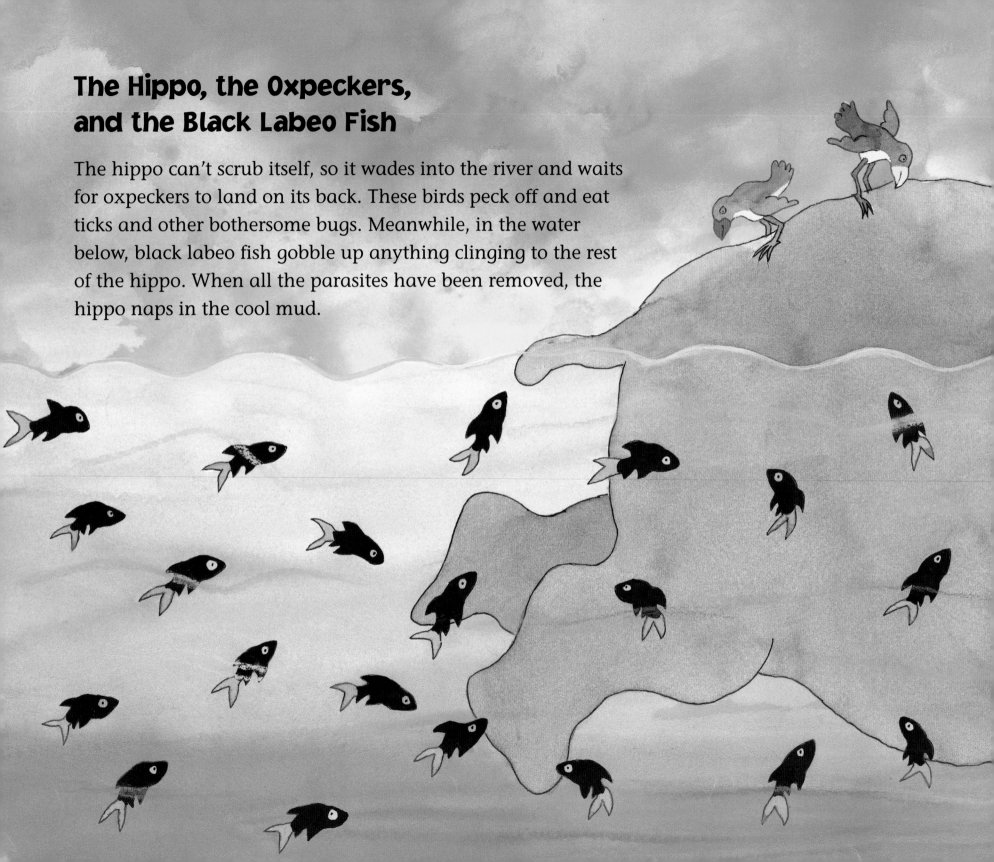

## The Wrasse and the Google-Eye Fish

When the wrasse is hungry, it dances on its head and wags its tail to announce that its cleaning station is open. Soon, lots of filthy google-eye fish are lining up for a bath. Like a small vacuum with teeth, the wrasse nips gunk from gills and scours parasites off scales. All the fish get a good washing, and the wrasse has a hearty meal.

# The Tuatara and the Sooty Shearwater

The tuatara is a slow and lazy reptile. It rarely even builds its own nest. Instead, the tuatara finds a sooty shearwater's cliff-top burrow and moves in while the bird is out.

But the tuatara is a good guest. It licks up every last slug, moth, worm, and beetle in the tunnel. When the sooty shearwater returns, the nest is clean, and the tuatara is welcome to stay.

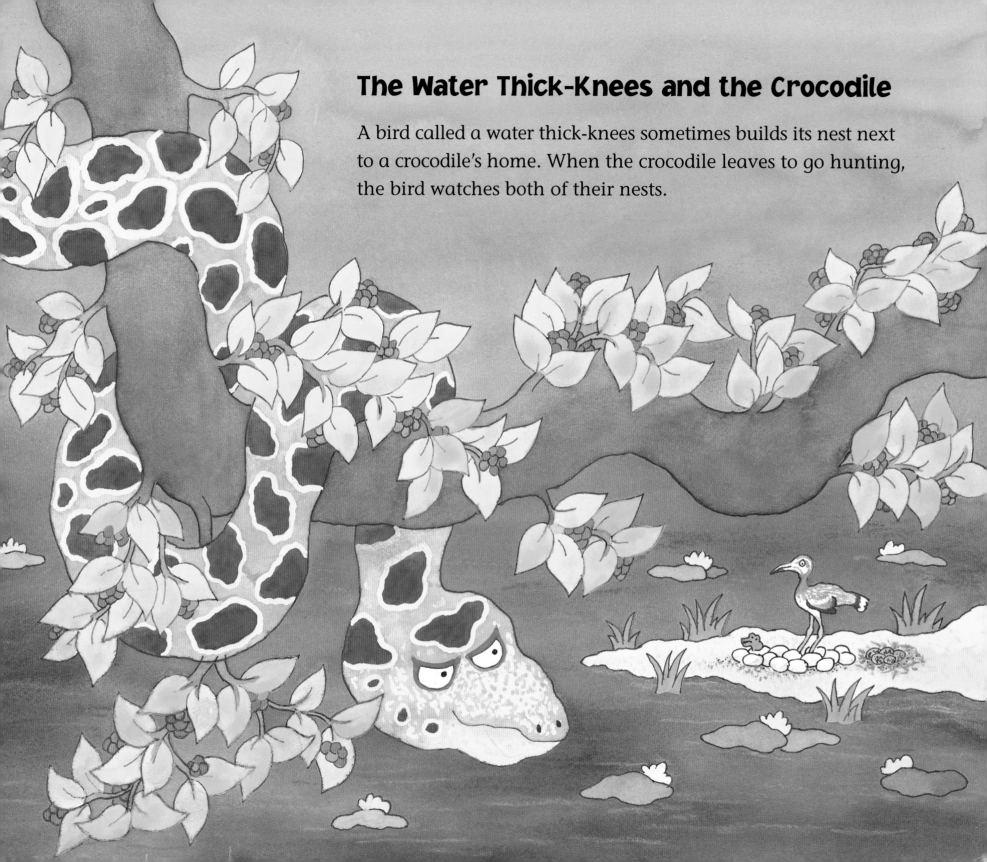

# The Water Thick-Knees and the Crocodile

A bird called a water thick-knees sometimes builds its nest next to a crocodile's home. When the crocodile leaves to go hunting, the bird watches both of their nests.

If trouble threatens the eggs or young in either nest, the bird screeches until the crocodile comes charging home. The water thick-knees and her family are safe beside their ferocious neighbor, because the crocodile will not eat its baby-sitter.

# Where You Can Find Weird Friends

Clown fish and some sea anemones inhabit the Indian Ocean. They are also plentiful in the western Pacific Ocean, where the blind shrimp and goby live. (All four are colorful residents of Australia's Great Barrier Reef.)

Hermit crabs and various other sea anemones exist together in many of the world's ocean waters. But certain hermit crabs in the Mediterranean Sea actually pick up anemones and put them on their shells.

The cleaning wrasse lives in nearly every ocean. The google-eye fish is present from the Red Sea, through the Indian and central Pacific Oceans, all the way to Easter Island.

Sperm whales encounter red phalaropes when they migrate through the North Atlantic Ocean.

The Portuguese man-of-war floats in most oceans. The horse mackerel is common in the eastern North Atlantic, although it also swims south along the coast of Africa, in the Indian and western Pacific Oceans, and in the Mediterranean and Black Seas.

Red ants and Large Blue Butterflies thrive among thyme blossoms during the summers of northern Europe.

Plovers clean a crocodile's teeth along the Nile.

Rhinos, cattle egrets, ostriches, zebras, impalas, baboons, hippos, and oxpeckers can all be found on the savannas and by the water holes of eastern and southern Africa. The black labeo fish inhabits nearby lakes and rivers.

The water thick-knees and crocodiles nest on riverbanks in southern Africa.

The forest mouse and beetles romp together through the rain forests of Costa Rica.

After several months at sea, the sooty shearwater returns to the rocky islands off the coast of New Zealand, the only place on earth where tuataras can be found.